Freedom in Networking

Freedom in Networking

A Story of Generational Wealth

Jonathan Sexsmith

YouSpeakIt
PUBLISHING
*The Easy Way
to Get Your Book
Done Right* ™

ISBN: 978-1-957972-01-5

This book is dedicated to my mother and late father,
John and Giselle Sexsmith.

Without you guys, I would not be who I am today.
I'm so grateful for everything you have taught and given me
and most importantly for teaching me to believe in myself, that I
could achieve anything I set my mind to and that
the power of the human potential is endless.

If it is to be, it is up to me.

PRAISE FOR
FREEDOM IN NETWORKING

"My love for network marketing as a lifestyle business is largely due to the incredible people it brought into my life. I'm delighted that Jonathan is keeping a generational torch burning brightly for the business his amazing parents built, one that has changed so many lives in the best of ways."

~ Lori Bush
Co-Founder & CEO at Solvasa LLC

"Jonathan Sexsmith reveals that most elusive of financial secrets: how to create and then successfully transfer wealth from one generation to another. His own story—born to a vivacious Puerto Rican mother and a highly disciplined Canadian father, both of whom wisely required him to achieve business success on his own—reads like Robert T. Kiyosaki's bestseller *Rich Dad, Poor Dad*. Readers of *Freedom in Networking* will have an advantage because he makes it clear that to achieve success in any field one must first learn to serve others."

~ Paul Alan Cox
TIME Magazine's *Hero of Medicine*
Goldman Environmental Prize winner

"Jonathan was turning 5 the year his father (John) had discovered networking. John's decision changed our life. Jonathan's book continues John's great legacy. I'm excited that this book will go on to positively change many more lives. A new generation goes forward.

Congratulations on your new book!" ~ Your mother

~ Giselle Gaudier Sexsmith
Owner at UBS
Internationally Known Networking Marketer
Lecturer, Teacher, and Author

CONTENTS

ACKNOWLEDGMENTS

I extend my deepest gratitude to the following people:

My incredible wife, Whitney, for simply being the most incredible, beautiful, caring, and loving human being I have ever met.

My parents for teaching me everything I know and giving me all the experiences necessary to master this amazing business.

All other life teachers who have crossed my path from coaches to teachers and countless friends—you all have impacted my life in ways that can't be imagined.

To the YouSpeakIt team for making this process one of the easiest, most fun processes I could have imagined writing a book.

And last but certainly not least, my incredible fox princes, Sir Lancelot and Sir Franklin.

INTRODUCTION

This book is about how to create financial freedom for yourself and your family by connecting to a platform allowing you to monetize a network globally with a networking business. It shares all the time-tested principles, from the perspective of one of the most successful assets that exist in the industry today. All the secrets to create a successful business for yourself and how our asset has withstood the test of time can be found within these pages.

Most people in the world have only learned the traditional way to make money, which is trading *time* for *money*. Typically, those who have money do not have any time because they work countless hours for their money.

Contrary to that, people who have a lot of time to enjoy the things they like typically do not have much money because they are not doing anything to generate financial benefits. We propose a different mechanism for generating income— leveraging the mechanics of wealth that can give time and money—which equals freedom. When you have the time and money to be with those you care about, you can be free to do whatever you want.

My name is Jonathan Sexsmith, and I am one of the only examples in the world of a successful transfer of a generational asset in the networking industry.

I am a second-generation wealth creator with one of the largest assets in the entire industry globally. Our asset is one of a handful that is not only surviving but thriving and has done so for almost forty years now.

One question I am often asked is: *How is this possible?* I want to share everything about it. I am one of the only successful transfers of a business in this industry to a son or daughter who has been able to manage to successfully take it over, work with the people, and continue to have it grow all over the world in over fifty countries.

How do you read this book for best results?

Find some quiet time for yourself with no distractions and read the book sequentially, chapter by chapter. Before you turn the first page, I want you to think about finding one idea from each chapter that can potentially change your life by showing how you can possibly add more time, become more financially free, or create harmonious relationships with other people.

I hope by reading this book you will see how to build a massive networking business and monetize a global network. I hope you gain insight into how to develop better mutually beneficial relationships with people. I hope it demystifies and clarifies some of the stigma surrounding the networking industry.

You deserve to have what you want, and there is a way for you to achieve anything you want if you are willing to take responsibility for yourself, make clear decisions, formulate a plan, work your ass off, and take action.

CHAPTER ONE

How I Got Involved in the Business

DISCOVERING I WAS AN ENTREPRENEUR

Entrepreneurship was a major topic of conversation growing up. My father taught me that an entrepreneur was someone who could evaluate their current condition and decide exactly what it was they wanted to change. An entrepreneur could match that decision with the deep burning desire of why they must achieve what they wanted and then, working relentlessly, break through brick walls to achieve it regardless of the naysayers or the adversity they must face.

An entrepreneur is willing to take risks, find comfort in being uncomfortable, and experience the pain that comes with going through what it takes to achieve their goals. An entrepreneur doesn't need motivation because they are disciplined and committed to relentlessly pursuing their end goal. I realized I was an entrepreneur as a kid when I came home one day and made the decision that I did not want to be fat anymore.

Fed Up

I was picked on every day because I was fat. I knew all the fat jokes in the world because I was the butt of them. I was about eleven years old when I came home from school one day, emotionally over it.

I walked into the kitchen and my mom, this tiny Puerto Rican lady, was standing in there cleaning dishes. "That's it," I said, looking at her. "I don't want to be fat anymore!"

Being a true Puerto Rican mother, she turned and said in her heavy accent, "Ay! Pero Juancito, you are so beautiful!"

It is funny to think about now, but back then it wasn't even close to a joke. I was tired of being made fun of and tired of being disliked for the way I looked. "No," I demanded. "I do not want to be fat."

At this time, I had also started to notice the ladies and realized my last name was Sexsmith, so I knew I needed to get my shit together if I was going to make *that* work.

How I Got So Fat

How did I get fat? It's not really rocket science—I liked to eat. To make matters worse, my mother had a hyperactive thyroid, which allowed her to eat whatever she wanted, whenever she wanted, and as much as she wanted. She thought her kids could do the same. I discovered that was absolute bullshit! Not to mention I am half Puerto Rican, meaning I love fried chicken, grape juice, and anything with sugar in it.

If anyone eats meals like that a couple times a week, they're done for. My snacks were composed of Shark Bites, Fruit Roll-Ups, Twinkies, Ho Hos, chocolate peanut butter wafers, cookies, M&M's, and Cheetos—everything we love but really shouldn't eat—and I would eat them all the time.

I used to make my mom take me to McDonald's to get a Fiesta meal, which had fifty chicken McNuggets, and I would eat them all. I would do this so often I discovered it was a scientific fact I needed thirty-two barbecue sauces for my meal to be thoroughly delicious.

"Mom," I would say as she inched forward in the drive through, "you know I need thirty-two barbecue sauces?"

She would look back and say, "No, I am not asking for thirty-two sauces."

"You better ask them for thirty-two barbecue sauces!"

"No way!"

She rolled down the window at the drive-thru and asked, "Can I please have a lot of barbecue sauce?"

"Thirty-Two!" I would scream, climbing my fat ass over the seats from the back of the car. "I need thirty-two sauces!"

How I Lost Weight

After I told my mom I didn't want to be fat anymore, she asked my father to help me. My father was a driven man. When it came to finishing a task, he was that type A, super alpha entrepreneur who got things done, but as a young optimistic fat boy, it never occurred to me I would be going to the gym with an absolute dictator. When I said I was not going to be fat, he was going to make sure I was not going to be fat every step of the way. It was his way or the highway.

He decided we needed to go to the gym. "Jonathan," he said, "we have to start exercising. I am going with you."

He told me to go to my bedroom and put on my *gym clothes*. I put on baggy shorts, a baggy basketball shirt, and came out. He yelled, "Hey, what are you wearing? We bought you gym clothes. Go and put on your gym clothes."

Fuck my life!

A panic came over me. I hurried into the room and saw these bright yellow spandex shorts that looked like bicycle shorts and a black spandex sleeveless tank top. *I look like a fat fucking bumblebee.* I was mortified, but I had to go to the gym in these clothes.

We went to the gym, warmed up, and began lifting weights. At the bench press, my dad went first and killed it. Of course, I thought: *This will be easy.* I started with the bar, and it weighed a million pounds. The minute I lifted it off the rack, my dad yelled all sorts of shit at me.

"Elbows in, chest up. You're doing it wrong! What the fuck? Didn't you watch me? If I can do it, you can do it."

I felt like I'd won the award for *Bench Press Idiot of the Year* and looked the part. My dad had enough of trying to *teach* me the weights and decided we would take an exercise class. Remember, this was in the eighties, the height of spandex, leotards, and leg warmers.

It turned out the exercise class was aerobics—stylized dance if you will. Picture a fat ass ten-year-old in spandex, shaking his shit with all the ladies in their leotards and leg warmers. Now picture his type A father doing it right next to him. Fuckin' weird, right? I sometimes still have nightmares about it.

My dad decided the class was a great workout and made me take it three times a week—with him. I will never forget what we did for our business at big events. We would host a party at the end, and when my dad danced at the parties, he did step aerobics as his dance moves. It was amazing.

Fast forward to me at twelve years old, 5' 8" and about 215 pounds—I needed a miracle. I tried every diet in the book.

The cabbage soup diet was one of the worst experiences of my life.

If I ever get the opportunity to meet the inventor of this diet, I'm going to kick him in his fucking balls. The soup tasted and smelled like sewage, and, of course, we were allowed to have as much of that as we wanted and then were only allowed to have certain things on certain days like three grapefruits. I managed to drop ten pounds, which was nothing, and gained twenty back.

I was *pissed!*

I then tried the no-fat diet. What a concept! If you don't eat fat, you don't get fat, right? Idiots! How did the mass media allow this to even be published? I must say I had a *magnificent* time on this diet. I was in fat-boy heaven. I was eating copious amounts of no-fat cookies, cakes, doughnuts, and ice creams. The sky was my limit.

Needless to say, this diet didn't work for obvious reasons—we know now but didn't know then—and I got fatter. My mom clearly thought I must have some disease and should be taken to the doctor.

They took me to our Hispanic family pediatrician, Doctor Rojas. I will never forget this: my mom took me, and both were speaking Spanish. I speak Spanish; I understand Spanish. They basically talked in front of my face about how fat I was. I thought: *This is great!* Then the doctor asked me to get on the scale.

If we are fat, stepping on the scale is the worst thing ever. We know we are fat; we don't need a scale to tell us. I got on the scale.

She looked at me and said, "Ay. Jonathan! You are so fat!"

Why don't you fucking tell me something I don't know?

Then they recommended I see an acupuncturist, a homeopathic doctor, to try different herbs and remedies.

My parents were sitting in the room with me while I was being evaluated, and I sat in front of this doctor as he asked a series of questions. I will never forget when he stared at my face, my mom sitting right next to me, and asked me if I shit regularly. *Umm what?*

"How often do you have a BM?" he asked.

I had no idea what he meant. I guess he wanted to get with the *street* lingo he thought the kids were using those days.

"Do you shit regularly?" he asked repeatedly, each time more flustered and aggressive. I was too fucking shocked to answer.

My mom was sitting next to me. "How fuckin' awkward is that?"

"You know what?" he asked. "Get on the table. We are going to do some acupuncture and fix your hunger."

In my mind, I thought, *fuckin' liar!*

He told me the needles would take away my hunger. The whole time on the table, I was wondering when I could leave so I could have my fried chicken sandwich. I left that appointment thinking: *I am never going back.*

I ended up learning the hard way that health was about balance. I wanted it so badly that, after trying diets and failing or gaining the weight back, I would try not eating and dropping weight only to gain even more back. I tried working out three times a day, seven days a week, but grew so sick and dehydrated I nearly went to the hospital. Not to mention, the gym was a scary place for a fat person. You wore tight clothes and looked ridiculous.

To this day, believe it or not, I still battle with my inner fat boy. Every now and again, I let him come out to play. A happy mind and body are a healthy mind and body. I am constantly attempting to embrace my genetics and stay on top of my health. I learned to make plans for my health and set ninety-day goals for what I'm going to achieve through all my hard work, determination, sweat, and sacrifice. If I don't reach my exact goals, do I freak out? No. I adjust my perspective and reset. But the truth is this:

If you fail to plan, you plan to fail.

Having gone through the pain of different diets and going to the gym, I realized there wouldn't be a quick fix. If I did not want to be fat, I needed to commit, decide, and be disciplined. It was not going to be something I could fix overnight. Through this journey, I dealt with pain and saw it through to the end, realizing if I could do it with my personal fitness, I could do it with anything. That is how I realized I was an entrepreneur.

HOW I LEARNED THE BUSINESS

Many people ask me how I got involved in the business: Was there something given to you? Were you handed this off? Why should we listen to and trust you?

I was born into it. I grew up in this business. When I was five, my father made me sit at house meetings every Saturday and take notes. The only products I used in my life are the products from this business. If you could see me through this book, you would see how pretty I am. I'm joking. Kind of.

Summer Cold Calling

One of my first real introductions to the business was when I finished high school. My father decided, for whatever reason, that I had the creativity, spark, and drive his other children did not have. I could easily learn and handle the business. All my other siblings tried at one point in their lives but never had success with it. Yet my father always believed I would.

When I was eighteen, he said, "You are going to stay home, and you are going to learn to do this business."

I learned it in what I personally consider one of the hardest ways possible. At the time, my father was looking to acquire a lead generation system. A company had given him qualified leads to test, so he decided I would spend my days cold calling and talking to hundreds of leads per day. Before beginning this task, he made me attend a certification course on our nutritional products to properly talk about the ones we sold.

After the certification, my dad said, "Jonathan, you are going to go into the office, and you are going to call a hundred leads a day, and when you are done, you can go off and do whatever you want to do."

I arrived at the office with a couple of scripts explaining what we were talking about at the time with a top questions list with the answers and a how-to-resolve rebuttals list.

I called a hundred people in two hours and said to my dad, "I am done. I called a hundred people, and I am going to go do my thing."

He was like, "Jonathan, you did not call a hundred people. That's impossible."

"Yes, I did."

"Jonathan, did you talk to a hundred people today?"

"Um . . . like talk? I left messages and made the calls."

He said, "You are not allowed to leave the room until you talk to every single person on the phone, no messages, no waiting for them to call back."

And I thought, *fuck my life!*

In hindsight, the experience taught me so much about how to successfully do this business. To speak with a person you don't know or have influence over is one of the hardest ways to involve someone in the business. That I was able to do it, especially at that age, gave me a tremendous amount of experience and made my father think: *Oh wow, this kid could do something.*

Discovering Working for a Living Sucked

Sometimes when you grow up in something so close to you, like a family business, you must do other jobs to realize what you want to do. When my parents started the business, they did it because they wanted to create a life they never had for their kids. My father grew up in a poor family. He was never formally educated and was seriously dyslexic. His major purpose when he started this business was to give his wife all of the things his mother never had and to give his kids all of the things he and his siblings never had. He did an incredible job at that! He always told us that because of this business, we would have the freedom of choice in our lives. We could pursue and do whatever it is we wanted to do in life because we chose to do it, not because we had to do it just to make ends meet.

If we wanted to be a doctor, lawyer, or astronaut, it wouldn't be because we needed a job to make ends meet; it would be because that was what we were passionate about and wanted to pursue. We had the freedom to choose, and I am eternally grateful for that.

I ended up pursuing different careers. I attended NYU, performed in Broadway musicals, acted in soaps, commercials, and on late night talk shows. Then I went into fitness. I coached trainers all over North America to be trainers themselves. I was in countless fitness publications nationwide and on television, but when I graduated from NYU, my father cut me off.

It was the first time in my life I had to work for a living and hated it. Guess what? Money runs out! When it does, I could not do the things I wanted to do, and if I wanted to make more money, I had to put in more hours. I woke up one day physically drained from teaching and training for endless hours every week, but I remembered conversations with my father about ways to create income for yourself. He taught me that most people on the planet made money by trading time for money whether it be working in fitness or drilling and filling teeth or seeing patients—people were trading time for money.

He also said there was another way people could make money—by leveraging the mechanics of wealth. The mechanics of wealth can be defined as offering someone an opportunity to be productive. Because you offer them the opportunity to be productive, you gain a cornerstone of that productivity. That is how all wealth in the world is created.

Normally, the only people who leveraged the mechanics of wealth were people who had a tremendous amount of capital, people who could invest in a business, build it up, and see it through, which was risky. But in our business, by monetizing a network, we leveraged the mechanics of wealth without tremendous capital and almost zero risk.

When I went to him to talk about doing something else other than what I was doing, he said, "Jonathan, if you project yourself five years into the future doing what you are currently doing, are you on track to having the life you want? Are you on track to spend time with the people you want to spend with and have the vacations you want to have and do what you want when you want?"

My answer was clearly no. So, we started to talk about how I could get involved.

Making a Decision

I was not on track to having what I wanted. I was stuck looking for something else. Of course, I remembered the incredible life my parents provided for me. I went to boarding school in Switzerland; I traveled and had the most amazing homes and vacations all over the world. We had my parents with us, spending time with us because they loved and wanted to be with us.

This lifestyle came from utilizing the incredible business vehicle they had, and that is what I wanted. At the time, it was a tough decision because I had talked to friends about the business, who had been on these vacations with me, who had been to our houses, and who knew all this was provided by this incredible business my parents started.

They would look at me and say, "No, that business does not work." It was infuriating to deal with.

I knew that by getting involved, I would deal with a lot of adversity. My dad ended up teaching me the basics: how to handle objections, prequalifying people, and closing. He said, "You must earn your place and respect in this business, and the only way you earn that in this business is doing it yourself. So, I will help you, but I am not going to give you a single thing. Our asset is willable, and if you prove yourself, maybe it could be yours."

He identified key people in our organization and asked me to work with them. In partnering together, we could achieve top-level recognition. If we did, I would be respected, trusted, and gain credibility, and then we could talk about how I could have a place in the family business. And that is exactly what I did.

I was one of the people that did it within the shortest amount of time as the fastest growing business in North America because I took it from zero to the top in eight months. My father was surprised. We had people calling and saying, "Jonathan, this is great." That was how it started. I took the challenge, bit down on it like a pit bull, and never let go. I saw it all the way through.

HOW TO THRIVE

Most assets with a thirty-year-old company do not continue. Over time, they dwindle and die. We are a unique representation of a situation in which that did not occur and have continued to grow, year after year, and we are growing more than ever.

Why? As technology changes, people are sometimes distracted and think the business tools created by technological advancement will build a business for them. They will bite so hard into one thing and look at the company from such a microscopic perspective that they lose the big picture of what this powerful vehicle is.

One thing we demonstrated for almost forty years is that the business is not about systems, technological tool advancements, or product packages—it is about the sound principles of the business. This is a people business. It is about human behavior, interacting with people in a meaningful way, and showing them how you can help them have what they want and contributing to their lives in a positive way.

These principles of human behavior will never change. They transcend cultures, countries, and languages. You can use technology to enhance these principles. However, biting down on technology and forgetting about those principles might provide a short-term gain but lack stability long term.

Building a Network Based on Trust

This business is about monetizing a network. When the wealthiest people in the world build a network, everyone else goes and looks for work. Build a network with integrity and trust. People do not care what you know until they know you care. Their bullshit radars are on high alert today, so if you come to them and they sense you are trying to swindle them, they will run like you have the plague.

Why? Because you will be operating with selfish interest. It is not about them and adding value to their lives. It is about your income, your bottom line, your sales for the day, and they won't want anything to do with you. It has been proven now more than ever that people do not like to feel like they are being sold to, especially by someone they do not know. Building a network based on trust and integrity comes from caring about the person and what they want, showing them how you can add value to their life.

Adding Value and Mutually Beneficial Relationships

The only way you can cultivate and monetize a global network is by adding value to their lives.

You must find out:

- What makes them tick and get up in the morning?

- What do they care about?

- How can you add value to their life in the form of income, lifestyle, community, more time, or a beneficial product?

It is a selfless endeavor, and sometimes people lose sight of that.

My father used to call it *teenager syndrome*. People will have a little bit of success and achieve a title or a big check, and suddenly they know everything. Their approach in the business becomes narcissistic. They lose sight of how they achieved their goal and what they gained. They talk more about their check, influence, and time on stage instead of what their customer wants and how they can work together to get them what they want. Then their business starts to dwindle.

When you add value to people, you can work in a mutually beneficial way. A positive relationship is a mutually beneficial one whether it's personal or professional. They are based on trust, kindness, integrity, and adding value to one another. When you focus on building those relationships by authentically wanting to contribute, you win all day long because then you can add value to them by showing how they can have what they want.

Showing People How They Can Have What They Want

When you are adding value for someone, find out what they want and show them a clear concise way you can work together to help them achieve whatever it is they want. It must be clear and authentic and have integrity. Otherwise, you are some sleazy salesperson trying to get them into something. If you can legitimately help them receive what they want, then your business will build stability and continue to grow. One reason we still do this and continue to grow today is that we 100 percent know we add value to others' lives. It feels amazing when you can speak to someone and genuinely hear what they want is something you can help them with.

Having a plan, you know in your heart and mind with complete faith that it works. You can work with the person to implement a strategy and see it work for them. For me, it is the greatest joy I have in this business.

CHAPTER TWO

Making a Decision to Do Something

WHAT IS A BURNING DESIRE?

Identifying your burning desire is the most important part in deciding to accomplish a goal. It will force you to break through walls to achieve it. It is the first step to manifesting the life and goals you strive for. Your action, habits, and behaviors will be firmly rooted and motivated by it.

My father used to quote Abraham Lincoln: *Always bear in mind that your own resolution to succeed is more important than any other one thing.* Here's another way to phrase it: The past does not matter, facts do not matter, obstacles do not matter, and adversity does not matter. It is only your decision and resolve to see that decision through to the end.

He asked, "Why do you get up in the morning and why should people care? What are you trying to achieve? What do you want out of this life?" I was taught that we have unlimited potential and can achieve whatever we believe if we have a burning desire to do it.

Through reading many books on human behavior, it has been shown that people do not make decisions and do things in their lives because their brain says they should do it. Everybody knows they should eat well—not guzzle sugary drinks—go to the gym, and exercise regularly. That does not mean they do it.

A burning desire cannot be a logical thing that makes sense to you. It must be something emotionally igniting. There are several emotional triggers for people. They can be fear based or spite based. People who end up achieving the goals they set for themselves normally have desire grounded in joy or love. They are emotionally connected to the work so that when they go through adversity, have had a bad day, or work hours away from their family, they remember why they are doing it and continue regardless of adversity.

There was a guy that wanted to find the secret to success, so he traveled all the way to Tibet because he was told a monk knew the secret to it. One day, the monk took him out to a body of water, grabbed him by the back of his head, and shoved him under. The guy was fighting back, thrashing and flailing, gasping for air. The monk finally pulled his head out of the water.

"What are you doing to me?" The guy screamed. "Are you fucking crazy?"

The monk shoved the guy's head back under to the point where the guy was going limp, but at the last second, the monk lifted him out and asked, "What do you want more than anything right now? In this moment?"

The guy cried. "I just want to breathe. Please stop."

The monk looked at him and said, "When you want success as bad as you want to breathe, then you will have a burning desire, and you will have success."

Having It Connected Emotionally and Intellectually

When you are only connected intellectually to achieving a goal, the minute life gets tough, it will not be enough to keep you going. It is why people give up. If the connection is superficial and disconnected from anything emotionally igniting, it will not push you toward manifesting everything you want. Be connected emotionally because you must look at yourself and evaluate your current condition, where you are right now and where you want to be.

It can be painful. The average person is not willing to look at themselves in that way. The bottom line: The real key to success is the burning desire—the intention—to win. Most people overlook intention because they are too worried about things they do not have. They think: *I do not have the personality, the contacts, the support, the looks, or talent.* When you have desire connected emotionally and intellectually, you want to win so much that none of the negative thoughts matter because you get up every single day thinking and dreaming about it.

Seeing Adversity as Opportunity

I recently acquired my Brazilian Jiu-Jitsu black belt. I have done martial arts my entire life and have quite a few belts, but this was the most arduous process I have ever been through. It takes on average about eight to ten years for someone to get a black belt in Brazilian Jiu Jitsu, and there are only about 5,600 people certified globally. It is one of the most challenging things I have ever done in my life but also one of the most rewarding accomplishments I have ever achieved. No matter what we try to accomplish, adversity will present itself.

In Brazilian Jiu Jitsu, the adversity that presented itself was more intense than anything I ever experienced: endless injuries, fractured wrists, dislocated shoulders, a blown-out knee, knee surgery, and a terrible MRSA infection that lasted six months. I had to deal with winning, but then suddenly losing in competitions. Then my father passed away, and I woke up countless mornings asking myself: *Why am I doing this? Why would I continue doing this?*

No matter what you do, you will encounter adversity and ask yourself the same questions, but you'd better have good answers or you will give up. My burning desire has always been so strong that it has never crossed my mind to quit.

Never. In Brazilian Jiu Jitsu, I planned to get my black belt even if it killed me. Nothing would stop me.

Whatever it is you are trying to accomplish, when you have a connected burning desire, it does not matter what happens to you. You will move mountains to achieve your goal. When you face adversity, instead of being a victim and wallowing in rejection, injury, and pain, and coming up with reasons why it would be okay to quit, simply look at them as bumps in the road, as learning experiences, and as opportunities to adjust.

DREAMS, GOALS, AND MENTAL TOUGHNESS

Dreaming Big

Unfortunately, we are often conditioned into thinking we should live smaller lives. We are told we cannot have the things we dream of having. We are told to be realistic, to get our heads out of the clouds, and that we're crazy for thinking we could have things we want to have and achieve.

As kids, we dream of having everything we want, but as we go through life, we realize it is not easy. Some people diminish our perception of the greatness we could possibly achieve, and because of that, most people dream too small. I have always believed if I can dream it, I can do it. I used to say that my dream was so big I would take over the moon and call it planet Sexsmith. People must reacquaint themselves with the notion that it is okay to have big dreams.

There was a seven-year-old kid who went to school, and his teacher gave an assignment to the class. The assignment was to write about their dreams of the things they were going to be when they grew up, the things that they wanted to have. This kid hands his assignment to the teacher, and the next day the kid looks at this paper and the teacher gave him an F. He was distraught and did not understand why.

He asked the teacher why she failed him. He did what was asked by the teacher.

"Listen, your paper was too much like fantasy," she said. "You can't have these things. Look at where you live. You live in this tiny town. Look at what your parents do. You can't have this life you wrote up in this paper, so you need to go back home and, if you rewrite this in a more reasonable way, I will re-evaluate your grade."

He went home that night and shared what happened with his mom. They talked it out, and he went back to school the next day. The teacher asked, "So did you rewrite the paper?"

"You know, actually I did not," he said.

She asked why he was going to keep the F.

"I am going to keep my F," he said. "You can keep this F on my paper, and you want to know why? Because I am going to keep my dreams."

I love that story so much because that is the attitude we must have. Regardless of our situation, our education, our background, and what happened to us in the past, never ever let anyone diminish or take your dreams from you.

Dreams to Reality

You must dream big, but to achieve those dreams, set clear achievable goals for yourself. *A dream without a goal is only a wish.* To manifest a dream into reality, create a blueprint of action steps by writing down clear, detailed goals. Set three main goals for yourself for whatever you plan to achieve.

Twelve-month goal. Look at where you are today. Twelve months from now, what is it that you want to achieve?

- Write it down and be specific.
- Write it as if you have already achieved the goal.
- Include the future date and time exactly twelve months ahead.

Now, imagine you have achieved the goal. Picture yourself in that success:

- Where are you sitting?
- What are you doing?
- What occurred relating to what you accomplished?
- What did exactly you accomplish?
- Who are you with?
- How do you feel about accomplishing this goal?

There has been a lot of information about writing down your goals in this fashion. Unleash the powers of the energy field that allows you to manifest things into your life.

Ninety-day goal. Write in the exact same fashion. Where do you want to be in ninety days from today? What have you achieved?

Thirty-day goal. Make a road map for the thirty days. Carve out time in your calendar and put in all the micro details of what you are going to do each day to ensure you will hit your thirty-day goal.

Mental Toughness

As you continually push yourself to achieve your dreams, you start pushing the boundaries of those around you as well. By moving out of your comfort zone, you start pushing people who are used to you being the way they believe you should be out of their comfort zone.

What happens? They talk shit about you and say you can't have or do these things. They try to take your dreams away from you. Often, your closest friends and even your family members are the ones who will say: *You can't do this.* Have mental toughness and guard your attitude with your life in the process of seeking your goals. You must be willing to achieve them with or without the people around you.

It is said your five closest friends will reflect your net worth. When you reach your end goal, you may not be in the same circle of friends you started it with. That's okay!

There is a saying: *It is harder to be mentally tough than it is to do eight hours of manual labor.* Why? Because being mentally tough and dealing with those external circumstances is not only physically challenging, it is also emotionally challenging. However, if you prepare for what could happen to you, you will not be shocked and won't quit. People will try to take your dreams away from you—they will say mean things, they will talk behind your back.

When that happens, are you going to give up?

I'll never forget a story frequently told about Winston Churchill and Lady Windsor. They were heavily debating, and, at one point, Lady Windsor looked at Churchill and said, "Winston, if you were my husband, I would put poison in your coffee!"

He thought for a minute, paused, and looked right back at her and said, "Well if you were my wife, I would drink it!"

That is the attitude you must have with the naysayers. Don't let it bother you. Guard your attitude with your life and simply move on.

ENTHUSIASM AND COMMITMENT TO EXCELLENCE

Vibrations—Enthusiasm Is Contagious

When you observe others, you will see those who pop out, who will catch your eye for some reason, and there are others who you would never notice. It has a lot to do with their zest for life and enthusiasm. All humans vibrate at thousands of vibrations per minute, and people pick up on it. When you live your life enthusiastically, you attract more positivity, more affluence, and more abundance. Enthusiasm is not enough alone because you still must do the work. But when you are enthusiastic, you can unleash your own unlimited potential.

There is a simple but life-changing formula for unleashing unlimited potential: You beat about 50 percent of the people on the planet by working hard. Then you beat 40 percent by standing for something and being an honest person operating with integrity. The last 10 percent of the people are as good and hungry as you are, and it is a fight in the free enterprise world. Working enthusiastically attracting abundance to your circle of influence makes beating out that 10 percent much easier.

Dealing With Rejection

Rejection is often the number one reason why people quit. Whether it is rejection from friends and family or personal rejection from feeling like you're failing, rejection can be detrimental and keep you from reaching your success.

My mom used to tell me, *If somebody says no to you about the business, high five yourself and know that you are one step closer to a yes.* My father was the first involved in the business. However, some things happened, and he decided he did not want to do it anymore.

At the time, my mom, who was against this business at first, had been taking me and my sister modeling in New York City. We were Ford models. We did a bunch of catalogs. I was the Lacoste boy, but she was able to take us because of the extra money from the business my father brought home. When he said he was not going to do it anymore, she said, "What?! Pero, this is good money!"

So, she decided to start doing the business, not really knowing much about it, but she knew there were great products and liked them. One day at the beach, she took my sister, Natalie, and me to the beach and met up with some friends. They were Yale graduates with MBAs, respectable, credible, high-level people.

"What is that?" her friend asked.

"Oh, this is my business," she said.

Her friend said, "What? Really? Well, we are always interested in opportunities. Why don't you come to the house and tell me and my husband what this business is about?"

She drove down to their house by herself and told them about the business. The husband of my mom's friend was a huge guy—6' 6", 300 pounds—a massive, intimidating character. My mom is a five-foot, little Latin woman. And she went on with lots of stories about how she took us modeling, how she had extra money to do this and that. She was enthusiastic and clearly excited. At the end of the meeting, the husband stood and looked at my mom.

"Well," he says, "Giselle, this was really fun. This was really entertaining, but I can see that you do not know anything about this business, so once you figure it out, why don't you come on back, and we will do this again?"

My mom went home and got my dad. They went down and presented the business again. Those people ended up involved in the business and achieving the top of the compensation plan. Had my mom not been so enthusiastic, had my mom not had that zest, energy, fun, and all those vibrations that made people want to be around her, they would have never invited her back for another meeting.

I share that story to illustrate the power of being genuinely enthusiastic—it cannot be fake. People pick up on the fake stuff and will run away from you.

Commitment to Excellence

Often, when you struggle and do not have the success you believe you deserve, the tendency is to point fingers and blame others. Well, if you are pointing one finger, blaming someone for your struggles, there are three other fingers on your hand pointing right back at you.

If something is not working out, be willing to look at your actions, habits, behavior, and beliefs. Self-examination is hard because we want to believe we are perfect. We do not want to be personally accountable for our shortcomings. We want to believe we are great and that we are doing everything right, especially if we try hard to achieve things. Regardless of what it is, there is always feedback you will receive through the process of doing.

If you are struggling, look at yourself and be willing to figure out what you are doing wrong. Be willing to take responsibility. In our business, feedback comes whether you make money or not.

My father used to tell me, "If you do ten presentations and get ten *nos*, you are doing something wrong. So, figure out what you are doing wrong."

There are only four things we do in our business, and these four principles, regardless of how technology and time progress, stay the same:

- Prequalification
- Presenting
- Closing
- Teaching others to do the same

You must be willing to become excellent at these things every single day.

Work on the areas in which you experience weakness, which means you must also be willing to work. There's a common saying that opportunity is missed by most people because it's dressed in overalls and looks like work.

No matter what you do in life, you are going to work. You can plan, dream big, and live enthusiastically, but if you do not meet these elements with the willingness to work your ass off, you will never find success.

CHAPTER THREE

Deciding Who You Are in the Business and How to Monetize a Global Network

WHO ARE YOU IN YOUR BUSINESS?

In this section, I will help people look at their networking business from a more macroscopic point of view to facilitate involving as many as possible.

People Label Entrepreneurs Differently

When you make the decision to start in the networking business, decide who you are in it, what you want out of it, and why you are going to add this extra work and effort into your life. To involve as many people as possible in the business, treat people with integrity and kindness and show them they can trust you. People do not care what you know until they know you care about them.

There are three questions people ask about you when you talk to them:

- Do you care for me?
- Can you help me?
- Can I trust you?

If any of those questions feel unresolved in their mind, people will not believe you and will likely not be involved in whatever you would like them to be involved. This is about deciding who you are, becoming a master networker, and knowing the different stories you share so you can connect with the person in front of you. Make sure you are giving them what they want and need while showing them how they can have what they want and need if they work *with* you.

How Much Effort Will You Give?

People label entrepreneurs with various titles, such as hustlers and boss babes, and often businesses give titles to work toward. Some companies use gemstone titles like Emerald, Diamond, or Platinum status. These titles can be more diminishing than anything else.

Your title in the business does not matter.

What matters is how much money you're making. Because you achieve the highest title in the comp plan does not mean you are making the highest amount of money. How you see yourself in the business is going to dictate the amount of effort you put in.

For example, if you see yourself as the master networker and CEO of your own business, the amount of work and effort you put into your business will be very different than if you see yourself as a side-hustle business, generating extra income weekly and monthly. How you see yourself is going to dictate what you do and how you are going to do it. This decision must be made before you start talking to people. You must have a clear blueprint of how you will achieve it.

The blueprint is simple:

Stage 1—The Formulation Phase

> This is the shortest but most critical stage. In this stage, you create your vision of the future and make decisions about your attitudes, habits, and action steps to achieve those plans and goals.

Stage 2—The Foundation Phase

> Most people start by building their business part time. In this phase, you typically do more work than you are getting paid for, but it is the most critical phase of your business.

Stage 3 —The Momentum Phase

> You have built such a solid foundation that you gain momentum. The length of time you spend in

momentum will be directly related to how much time you spend in your foundation phase.

Stage 4—The Stability Phase

This is typically where a lot of mentoring, teaching, and guiding others occurs.

Master Networking

What is a master networker?

My father defined a master networker as someone who sees everyone they come across as the next best entrepreneur in the world. He would talk to them, trying to involve them and their entrepreneurial potential by showing them how to add value to their lives.

This approach requires learning some basic skills. My father never went to college and was severely dyslexic, but they said his business gave him two degrees—an MBA and a PhD. In this business, the PhD comes first because the PhD is in street psychology and learning how to deal with people. Once someone masters how to deal with people, finding out what they want and showing them how they can have what they want, then they earn their MBA—a mega bank account.

A master networker can find out what people want, show them how they can get what they want, and how they will work with them. If you are a master networker, you will add value to their lives whether it is in the shape of having more time, money, or freedom to do whatever it is that they want with the people they want or in the form of using a better product to live better and longer.

Being a master networker has everything to do with the stories you tell because a networking business is customized entrepreneurship–everyone wants different things. Be equipped to tap in to what they want and have stories ready that match, showing them how they can what they want once they are connected to the networking vehicle. It's a different headspace to live in than having a product you are trying to sell to a consumer.

CUSTOMIZED ENTREPRENEURSHIP

When people are introduced to a networking business, it is often by the way of a product introduction. They try a product or see a demonstration, go to a home party, or maybe see a post online. It is a micro way of doing the business because it comes down to selling one product. Sometimes people are pigeon-holed into thinking this is the only way to do the business because it is how they were introduced.

When you can take a step back and see the business as a networking business, where you are connecting people to a platform and allowing them the ability to monetize in a variety of ways, you see a breathable space that is more all-encompassing. You deal with less objection along the way because there is more room for a variety of different people ranging from CEOs of companies to people looking for extra work. You are matching wants and needs versus trying to convince someone to buy a product—which is when you deal with a lot of objections, a lot of rejection—and that can cause people to quit because they feel stuck.

Thirteen Stories

Your stories will go from big and all-encompassing to smaller niche stories. Your stories will always change and evolve due to technological advances and macroeconomic circumstances. The number one all-encompassing story you can lead with is: Do you want to build a massive global network that can be a generational asset? I am living proof that it is possible for people to do.

1. The other day, I watched an interview with Kevin Hart talking about the reason why he keeps working. He is a comedic billionaire. The reason he continues to do what he does is to create a generational asset for his kids. It is a major trend people care about.

2. Two hundred million incomes are being taken away by technology, and we are seeking a solution to replace them. We see it in the news all the time. Just recently, HSBC laid off 35,000 middle management employees because technology replaced their positions. At this point and time, these people with college degrees and good salaries didn't prepare when asked, *What would happen if you lost your job?* They

always thought: *That will not happen to me. I did all the things that I am supposed to do. I went to college. I got a good job, and I have my family.*

Yet did they have a plan B? Suddenly, with the ways the world and technology have evolved, they are looking at that situation. Do they have a plan to replace those incomes? This is a major topic people can talk about.

3. Do you want to be a master networker and find out what people want and show them how they can have it to create a global network? Do you want to use an incredible financial vehicle that fits at the forefront of major trends so you can capitalize on massive global turnovers economically and get paid from several countries globally?

4. Use the mechanics of wealth versus trading time for money. Most people never learn about the mechanics of wealth and leverage income because they do not teach this sort of stuff in schools. You have to find somebody who does it, who knows it because the number one way people generate income for themselves is trading time for money, whether that is a doctor seeing patients every fifteen minutes, a dentist that is drilling and filling, or when I was working in fitness training clients. It is trading time for money.

Is there another way? What if you could get paid from countries all around the world? Is that something you might be interested in? You can also talk about the platform revolution and the opportunity economy. Everybody talks about the opportunity economy and the gig economy and how those appeals to huge demographics looking for something a little extra.

5. Looking back at the previous stories, you can see how they are getting smaller and smaller—more niche, right? As the master networker, you must know who you are talking to, so you know if this is what they are looking for. If the person is driving Uber as a side hustle currently, maybe they would be interested in this too. Huge trends today are life sciences, artificial intelligence, augmented reality, and the internet of things. There are many companies currently working with products in this area. If you are connected to companies like these, you can talk to people who are interested in these sorts of things, about those specific things, and how they can capitalize those industries macro-economically.

6. You can talk about organic. You can talk about controlled environment agriculture and traceable ingredients and how clean ingredients are defined. Some people who are not organic or vegan won't buy that. If you are not versed in talking about it, they will completely write you off.

7. You can talk about mega trends in general. What are the current mega trends? Whether your company is into anti-aging, devices, or technology, ask: How does that business vehicle fit perfectly in front of those trends, so you can capitalize financially?

8. You can talk about device platforms. Companies are coming out with all sorts of devices. If the company is worth itself, they should have patented and proprietary products that do things nothing else in the industry can do. When they give results that no other product in the world can give, you end up with a *blue ocean* strategy. Let me explain what the terms blue ocean and red ocean are. *Red ocean* occurs when there are lots of sharks in the water feeding on few little fish; it is a saturated business space. *Blue ocean* occurs when you are the only shark in the water. If you are working with a company that has patented and proprietary products, you have a completely blue ocean business space to capitalize on, and some people might be interested in capitalizing on it as well.

9. You can talk about customization and boutique product lines tailored specifically to certain demographic things, such as men or hair care lines. Start digging down into the real kind of micro different products lines.

10. You can talk about leaving the world a better place than you found it, contributing to peoples' lives in a positive way and being a force for good. Providing solutions for people to leave the world a better place might make them tick. Some companies have humanitarian efforts where proceeds of products go to different humanitarian efforts.

11. You can talk about social media and social selling. For a long time, there has been a buzz war about posting photos online, selling and retailing, and building a business. Where are you buying product wholesale yourself from the company? Retail it to people throughout the country and develop a customer base in that way.

12. People still go door to door. I know people that take ten days a month to focus on different areas and knock on doors to sell products. People still do that and if this is something that somebody wants to do, you need to be able to show them how to do that.

13. You can do product demos. Meet in coffee shops, throw home parties, and invite people over. Bring people to your house and have some food out. Talk product demos if that is what you like to do. There is a place for you in this sort of networking business.

You must fundamentally decide who you are first and what you want to do and then be able to show whoever is in front of you how they can also participate in a way that is meaningful to them. If you go through some of those stories and see how they go from big to small, you will see how you can involve people through all walks of life as if you know how to talk to them in a way that is meaningful to them.

Introduction to Prequalification and Closing

To find out how you need to talk to the person you are trying to involve in your networking business, you need to do what we call and have referred to in the past as *prequalification*. It simply means finding out what the person wants and if they are looking for something right now. Ask if it is the right time to get involved if you showed them how they could participate in something that could move them toward what they want.

Then there is *closing*. How are you going to close the person sitting in front of you? How are you going to get them to put pen to paper, sign up, and then purchase a product they would like?

Otherwise, these networking businesses are commission based. If you enroll people in your business and they do not buy any product, the commission is zero dollars. It does not matter the percentage of commission you are paid. If you are generating zero dollars through your network, you are paid nothing. Inevitably you must move some product through your organization, so you must develop the skills to do that.

MONETIZATION OF THE NETWORK

I will explain some fundamentals of how we have successfully monetized our network in over fifty countries in hopes that these principles can help you in some way.

Matching Needs and Wants With a Vehicle

You must find out what the person you are talking to needs and wants, and then show them a vehicle they can use that is real, that they believe in, and that they can have.

There are two parts to the brain: the limbic brain and the analytical brain. The analytical brain is facts and figures.

This part of the brain, even though things might make sense to you, is not what helps you make decisions. They found that the limbic brain is the decision maker. This part of the brain is tapped into storytelling. To activate the decision-making part of the brain, tell the person stories because the people that cared about them—typically their mother, father, or siblings—told them stories as kids. It lowers their defenses and makes them more likely to listen to you because, subconsciously, they already believe you care about them.

Prequalification is largely about sharing stories with the person—for example, why you became involved or what you're a part of—so they inevitably share stories with you about what they want and need, what they want more of in their life, and what they do not like about their life.

How can you lead into a conversation about how you are part of an amazing platform they can connect with?

It is about being able to share stories so their defenses lower and they are more inclined to share stories right back with you. That leads to a productive conversation to match the needs and wants with the vehicle.

Adding Value

This all comes down to people not caring what you know until they know you care. They want to know you can add legitimate value to their lives. If you cannot add value, they will not listen. Nobody will. People's bullshit radars are supercharged today. They can smell bullshit from ten thousand miles away.

People never like to feel they are being sold something, and they certainly do not want to be sold anything by someone they do not know. If they sense you are trying to con them into something for your own benefit, trying to make a sale or push a product on them, they are gone. They will not give you the time of day.

Approach them in a genuine way that adds value to them. Do it in a way that comes from finding out what they want and explaining how you can contribute to their lives in a positive way.

If you can convey that appropriately and work with a reliable and successful partner, you can win. It comes down to how you can increase their life joy in some way, shape, or form. If not, you are done. Forget it.

Prequalification and Closing

There are fundamental things every human wants: love, spirituality, affection, and freedom. If someone is going to sit with you for a presentation or engage in a conversation about getting involved in a business, you need to address that you know what they are looking for. Is it generational wealth, supplemental income, time freedom, more travel, or starting something new? When you identify what the person is looking for, you will know exactly what to talk about.

I never present the business until I know why someone is sitting down to hear about it. I need to know what makes them tick, what they are looking for, or if they want to make ten thousand dollars a month so they can save extra for their kids' college fund. If this is what they want, I will talk about that college fund during the entire presentation, to show them how I can do that.

When it comes to closing, I will ask them if I showed them a viable way for them to participate with me and work together to show how they can put their kids through college and not have extra stress.

In closing, you are going to deal with objections.

There are two types of objections that arise when you are closing somebody:

- *Misunderstanding.* Maybe they did not understand something you said through your presentation or something more specific about a compensation plan.

- *Valid Objection.* We always teach people that an objection is simply a request for more information, so do not be afraid of the objection. It is not a no. They are asking for more information.

When I first got involved in this business, I would become frustrated and upset after the end of the presentation because people would look at me and ask if it was a pyramid scheme. I would become angry, but I learned that I must look at them like children and think: *They do not understand. Take a deep breath, have some patience, and figure out how to move the process forward.*

In handling the objection, one rule of thumb is to never answer a question with a yes or no. Validate their objection, ask if you heard them properly, and then try to resolve that objection by asking them to agree with you.

For example, somebody might ask me, "Isn't this just a pyramid scheme?"

I would say, "That is a great question. Please tell me, what do you know about a pyramid scheme?"

I let them tell me everything they know or do not know about a pyramid scheme.

I would then say, "These are valid concerns. You have every right to be concerned about that because those things are terrible."

At this point, I would present examples of what I know about the industry, the business, and ask them, "Do you agree with me?

Would you agree a company that is a publicly traded on the New York Stock Exchange, recognized by Forbes magazine, won accolades in several publications for best products in the world, and has a track record of creating millionaires from the inception of the company until today is not an illegal company? Most of the time they will agree with me.

"Great. This resolves your concern. Let's get you started." If they say no, then I will ask another question and handle it in the same way.

Prequalification and closing are tied together because people typically only remember the beginning and end of what you show them, and you only have a limited amount of time with people. You must connect to the reason why they sat down— the prequalification—to how you are closing them and ask them if you showed them a viable way to get what they want. When you become better at prequalification and closing, you will have more success in the business.

People always say, "Closing is so scary. Asking someone to sign up and when are they going to buy something is so scary."

Well, you are either going to do it or not because life is hard. You must choose your *hard*: being broke is hard, not having time is hard. Not having the freedom to do what you want with your kids or spend time with your family is hard.

You know what? Making money is hard. Closing people is hard. Building a business is hard. Choose your *hard*. So yes, closing is hard, but are you going to learn to do this and confront it and make it work or are you going to be content where you are?

That is your choice.

People will also say they do not want to be pushy, but I tell them they should never feel like that. Nobody likes to feel like that, and you are probably going to think: *This person will never talk to me again*. It is not being pushy—but maybe a little *nudgy*.

I relate this story about an alligator to closing.

There was a billionaire that threw a party many people attended. He told everybody to go out back to the pool. In the pool, he had huge alligators. He stepped outside and announced to the party, "Okay, guys, I will give somebody $10,000 if they jump in this water and swim across this pool."

Nobody jumps in.

Then he said, "I know this is scary, but I will give somebody $50,000 if they jump in this water and swim across this pool."

Nobody jumps in.

Then he said, "You know what? I am going to give somebody *a million dollars* if they jump in this pool and swim across."

Bam!

Somebody was in the water, swimming as fast as they could, and the alligators swam after him, chomping and snapping. He got to the other side unscathed and climbed out of the pool while these alligators chomped at his feet.

The billionaire says, "My goodness, that was the most incredibly brave thing I have ever seen. You know what? Forget the million dollars. I am going to give you whatever you want because that was unbelievable."

The guy looks at him and says, "You know what, man? I don't want anything like that. I just want to know who pushed me."

Closing can be scary. It's scary not only for you but also for the person. As the person goes through their fear and gets through it, you never know what rewards will be at the end of it.

CHAPTER FOUR

Industry Misperceptions and Your Relationship as a Leader With Corporate Executives

INDUSTRY TABOOS

There are blanket assumptions made about this industry.

Whenever you join any business, it is your responsibility to do your own due diligence, to find out as much about the company possible, and to make sure you fully understand what you are getting involved in.

As you investigate the trustworthiness of the company you are looking to partner with, ask some important questions:

- How did their top leaders generate their income?

- Is it the same compensation plan you are joining?

- Did they do the work the way you have to or were they first in and grandfathered without having to build like you do?

- Do they make most of their money from product sales or from selling training materials?

- Do they have legitimate products?

- Do the products work?

- Are there any relevant scientific studies supporting their claims?

- Do they require purchases to get paid?

- Do they pay solely based on recruiting?

Look at the compensation packages of every single company you are considering attaching your network to. Find out how they pay. Are the levels capped at an appropriate level? The sweet spot is typically six levels. If it is deeper than that, it could potentially be a bit sketchy.

Choosing a Trustworthy Partner

It is unfortunately typical when somebody joins a networking company and starts to talk to their friends or family about it that their peers will exclaim that they have been conned into a pyramid scheme. They will hear words like *multilevel marketing* or *network marketing*, triggering a terrible reaction. Often, they have never been involved in the industry at all and have only seen sensational headlines about bad actors in the space or heard a friend got involved with something that didn't have success. They have a negative association with the industry without really knowing anything about the industry.

It is important to understand fundamentally that, in any industry, there are good actors and there are bad actors. Unfortunately, when this industry began, it was not regulated and, at one point in time, about 200 networking companies started every year in the USA. It was wild. In a positive way, it illustrated the power of the business model and leveraged income, but in another way, it allowed unethical people to do highly unethical things.

First and foremost, personal accountability and responsibility are paramount. You are a grown adult and responsible for your own situation. Do your due diligence and research anything you choose to get involved in. If you do not do your research and get involved in some crazy company, that is your fault. You did not take the time to understand what you were getting involved in.

I recommend this checklist to find out what makes a viable company today.

1. Are they publicly traded? If they are publicly traded, you can have confidence it is a legitimate company.

2. Do they have accolades about their payment processes to make sure they pay on time and have impeccable accounting?

3. Does the company have a track record for success? How long has the company been around? Are there new people making money today and having success?

4. Do they have proprietary and patented working products that are substantiated with clinical trials, double blind clinical trials, or better?

5. What accolades/awards does the company have?

6. Are their levels capped appropriately?

What typically ends up making a company a pyramid scheme is a dwindling pool of money where only the people at the top make the money because the levels aren't capped. In this situation, there isn't enough money to pay out to everyone. The good actors in the industry cap the levels at an appropriate rate where new people can come in today and make more money than the people who started at the beginning.

Red flags you should be aware of:

- Pyramid schemes often do not have products.

- If they have products, they do not work, and there is no substantiation behind the claims that they make.

- Company pays solely on the basis of recruiting people without any products sold.

- Contract requires monthly purchases or fees to sign up.

It's entirely ridiculous to hear the term *Network Marketing* or MLM—*Multi Level Marketing*—and assume it is all bad because that simply is not true. Whenever you assume anything, you make an ass out of you and me.

Today, the networking industry is one of the most regulated industries by the FTC because once they find the bad actors in the space, the companies are shut down. Sometimes when you Google names of the bigger companies in the industry, you will find a lot of garbage, but not all of it is true.

Weed through people who are disgruntled and did not make it or are working with another company and leaving negative reviews. Differentiate the noise online to find out what is credible and real about the business you are thinking of partnering in and then move forward. There are people who build businesses ethically and with integrity, but there are those who don't. Luckily, those who don't inevitably get shut down. However, one rotten apple is not a reflection of the entire industry or salesforce.

The 1 Percent Rule

Many times, when people are trying to involve their network in a networking business, some will object and say, "Oh yeah, but you know what? I have looked at their income disclosures, and only 1 percent of the people in the business actually make good money." It's funny to me that in this industry, it's a huge faux pas, but that statistic holds true for any industry you consider in the world. It is only 1 percent of the entire global population that makes over a million dollars a year. It does not matter what industry you are a part of; this statistic is always going to be the case. For some reason, in network marketing, people want to say that fact makes it a scheme or a scam.

If I hear this, I always tell people this story about when I went to school at NYU for music and theater. My program was in the top five in the country for performing. It was and still is one of the most expensive schools in the country. I spent hundreds of thousands of dollars on this education to be a performer. I worked for a good amount of time after college but did not make close to the amount of money I spent on my college tuition.

If I did a business analysis on my investments in the entertainment industry, I would be completely bankrupt, but somehow it is accepted as okay to be in a huge amount of debt with no certainty you will financially make that money back if you remain in that industry.

Most people in entertainment with degrees from amazing universities end up supporting themselves as waiters or bartenders, but for some reason this is socially accepted. I would also say it's more like .01 percent of the entire industry that truly reach *the top* and find fame and fortune.

But there is no real stigma attached to this. A big criticism of network marketing is, in some companies, you must *invest*, which normally means you buy a package to start your business. In good companies, you are not required to buy a package, but it is normally recommended so you can familiarize yourself with the products and find out if they're good and if they work, so you can talk about what you like about them. You will be more confident that the company is real, that it has good products, and that the customer will receive effective products for their money.

We aren't talking about a huge investment. I have seen packages ranging from thirty to a thousand dollars, and you can normally pick what you like.

Any business you start will require startup money. Whether you start a franchise, a gym, or a local shop, or even if you only want to be a realtor or trainer, you must invest in your licenses and training with no guarantee you will ever sell a house or have any clients.

Most realtors who spend the money to get their licenses are out of the industry in two years, but there is no real criticism of their requirements. When you look at what the startup cost is in a networking business, the risk is next to nothing, and most of the good-acting companies will have a money back guarantee policy for returning products. The bottom line is that only 1 percent of any industry will be successful.

My father taught me the 1 percent rule could be defined as follows:

1. Most people go through life simply wishing for things, and those wishes are fickle—they come and they go. They have no power to shape anything or control their destiny, and this number of people who simply wish for a better life is about 70 percent of the population.

2. A small percent of that 70 percent actually develops their wishes into desires. They want the same thing constantly but that is the end of their commitment. This is about 10 percent of the seventy percent.

3. Some develop their wish into desires and then into hope, which means they dare to imagine, and from time to time they accomplish and achieve things, and this is probably about 8 percent of the 10 percent.

4. About 6 percent are able to translate their hope into genuine belief, and they expect what they want will actually happen.

5. In my experience, about 4 percent will then crystallize their wishes, their desires, their hopes into belief and then into a burning desire and finally into certainty.

6. It is only 1 percent that will take the next step and actually make a plan to get what they want and execute that plan. They apply their belief, their certainty, and their positive mental attitude and expectation and have a relentless work ethic until they achieve what they want. That is the one percent, no matter the industry.

LEADERSHIP AND CORPORATE EXECUTIVES

Roles and Responsibilities

Let's talk about leadership. They are the revenue creators generating all the revenue for the company. They are responsible for attaching networks to the opportunity platform and cultivating networks—training and teaching them how to do the business ethically and responsibly. They also hold meetings and events and mentor people through their life in the business to have success.

The main departments that matter in the company on the corporate side:

- Finance
- Accounting

- Compliance
- Research Development
- Global Marketing
- Supply Chain

We have lived through more than six CEOs at our company, and it does not change anything with the business. There is a division called Market Management that most newer companies are eliminating because the positions cause more problems than positives in the business. Technology is already at a point that they can be completely replaced, meaning the company can operate more efficiently, cut high management salaries, and place that money elsewhere.

The reason market management—in which you have presidents of different markets, head of global sales, or VP of sales—conflicts with the leadership at certain times is because they do not sell anything. We do. They do not recruit, train, or hold meetings. They do not attach networks to the company.

So, what do they do? These positions were artificially created to further internal corporate politics because they are glorified note passers giving feedback from top leadership in their regions to the C-level executives. There's no need for this anymore because in a global business where you are a master network attaching people all over the world to an opportunity platform, regional and geographic limitations have no place. Placing a person who has never built a business like this as a decision maker for a region is nonsensical, causing delays and inhibiting growth in a networking company.

As a leader, when you are having success, your market president or GM might offer things to you, but remember that there is no real value added to your organization from that department. Don't get big-eyed and think you need them or that you're special because they have a corporate title as president of a region. They do not add value to your business and can simply try to use you to get into your network, to cause fractures in the organization, and to cause leaders to fight with one another.

Staying in Your Own Lane

We, the leadership, are not product creators. We are not scientists. You might find a leader that starts going crazy about how they are so sure they need this product in their market, and the company needs to make this product. That is not our place. Sure, we can test products and give feedback, but the companies are the ones spending on the endless research. Internal teams work every day to stay at the forefront of trends and develop products that fit in front of those trends to optimize our compensations.

We stay in our lane of attaching people to the opportunity, showing them how they can have opportunity and how we can add value to their life, showing them how they can be a part of this and have success. On the flip side, the corporation must stay in their lane which, unfortunately, they do not do.

That is why most companies are getting rid of them, but they often try to get involved with the leadership and try to train leaders on what they are supposed to be doing, how they think they should do the business, and how they should sell a package. *This is going to grow the business*, they think. All that is bullshit because they never move the needle of our business. Packages, trip incentives, and corporate-led events have never and will never move the needle. All these *perks* do is create friction between the leadership and corporate executives.

Also, if you have never built a networking business yourself, you can never in your life teach someone else how to. The only people who can teach you how to do this business effectively are those who have done it. The market management have never done it.

Why would you ever listen to their opinion?

INSULATING YOURSELF FROM THE NOISE

There can be a lot of distractions within the business and, if you give them too much attention, can cause disruption and inevitably cause people to want to quit if they feel unsuccessful. Always remember that someone else's success is not your failure. Everyone grows at their own pace in this business and if someone reaches success quicker than you, their speed does not mean you have failed, are doing something wrong, or that you won't find success yourself. If you ever feel like you are distracted, always come back to the reason why you started. That reason should be posted on your refrigerator and bathroom mirror, so you see it every day.

Go back to your goals. You should have what we call an OIC chart, which stands for *Organization Information Chart*, but also OIC is like, *Oh I See*, where you can keep track of your appointments, your calendar, and who you are working with. Put the focus back on you, your intention, what you want, where you are, and what you need to do to progress.

Take your intentions away from the noise of management and put them back on yourself. When you put them back on yourself, you will find yourself back in control of being able to make a change so you can make progress and have success.

Incentive Trips and Packages

The number one indicator of your success in this business is how much money you are making. It is not your title; it is not trips you have qualified for or other incentives the company might offer. You need to focus on productive actions that generate income for yourself. Income is why most people end up joining.

Sometimes the *sales team* within the company will start promoting incentive trips or different packages, and some people will build to qualify, using the packages the company created because the packages are discounted. Often the leadership doesn't realize that those packages are discounted because they're taking commission from the leadership to subsidize a cheaper price. So, you end up doing activities and selling certain things to qualify for something, but you are making much less money than you would have been.

My father always said, "If you want this incentive they're promoting, whether it's a car, a trip, whatever it is, let's figure out how, with this compensation package, you can generate enough income to get whatever it is you want. If it's a trip, let's leverage the comp plan and make the money so that you can go on whatever trip you want, wherever you want, with whomever you want." We will do that working with the products or services the company provides that will generate the most income for you and your family, and then you aren't losing commission by promoting an incentive package.

Again, don't get distracted by their noise. Someone may say to you, "I qualified for this incentive, did you?" You didn't, but you might be making five times more in your check than that person. It's customized entrepreneurship: stay focused on what you want and build in the way that makes the most sense to you in which you make the most amount of money for you and your family and don't care what anyone else is doing.

Crossline Groups

As you are building, you will sometimes hear about other groups starting to find success. Maybe if you are not currently having the success you want, you will look at what they are doing and think they have something you don't. That shift will distract you. The world is flat, and information is transparent. Other groups don't know anything that you don't know, so put the focus back on yourself and get back into money-generating activities.

Always remember, the only people who have a vested interest in your success are those in your upline. If you choose to work with people from other organizations, be mindful that it doesn't turn into you doing work for other people that doesn't add money to your bank account. You must trust people you are working with and stay focused on your goals.

The fundamentals and basics of this business will never change. Even if technology changes and different tools are used, the fundamentals will never change because they are rooted in human behavior. The tools should facilitate making the basics easier. No other group is going to know things you don't, so trust your process, your journey, and the people you are working with. Find ways to adjust, adapt, and make the business work for you in a way that makes you happy.

Trusting People You Work With

What moves the business, opportunity, or product? The number one product a networking company has is their compensation package. Fundamentally, it's all based on utilizing an amazing financial vehicle to get what you want. The opportunity and product sales live together synergistically. It is never one or the other. They are equal partners.

You will find people who want to be involved in the opportunity, and you will find people who simply want to be satisfied consumers. It's all part of the business, and there is space for all of it. It is up to you as a master networker to be versed in all of it, so you can deliver to the person in front of you what they want and need. It's never one product launch or one product that will drive the business.

You must look at the future of what's coming to show others how they can participate with you. The business grows when you add other entrepreneurs to it. The only way to add more entrepreneurs is by showing them a future story of what's coming and why they should become involved now so they can capitalize on all the amazing things occurring.

Building with the hype of one product launch to the next and trying to limit information from others about the future of what's coming is detrimental to your business. You put yourself in a saturated business space of being another guy selling some product. Yes, product launches are important; however, you must pair launch offerings with the future of the business to be able to involve more entrepreneurs in your business.

Chapter Five

Beliefs Needed
to Achieve Success

WHAT ARE YOU HOLDING ON TO?

It has been said that humans are born with two fears: the fear of loud noises and the fear of falling. All other fears are self-created. Those fears can be limiting and paired with subconscious limiting beliefs that set people back and don't allow them to achieve their full potential.

There is a region in Africa where the villagers and farmers eat baboons because it is all they have for protein. They trap them by drilling a hole in a tree large enough for a baboon to slide a hand into and place a macadamia nut inside. Baboons, they learned, love macadamia nuts. Once a baboon closes a hand around one, the hole will be small enough it cannot pull its hand out. It wants the macadamia nut so badly it will never let go, even as it sees hunters coming toward him knowing it should run away.

What macadamia nut are you holding on to?

We all have our own macadamia *nuts*. They are the limiting beliefs we don't even know we have. We need to be aware of what beliefs and thoughts we hold on to that might need to be released to realize our full potential. Identify and recognize your negative self-talk, acknowledge it, and find out why you talk to yourself that way. Then look at what is occurring around you. When you do that, you will gain the ability to place yourself in the present.

Nine times out of ten, the limiting beliefs and negative self-talk we hold on to are not real. They have been subconsciously programmed in us through negative experiences. Until you acknowledge and address those thoughts, you are not free to let them go. Most people go through their lives without even knowing they are holding on to limiting beliefs. That is why they lack the success they are looking for.

Belief

When you believe in a thing, you must believe in it all the way, implicitly and unquestionably.

~Walt Disney

When you believe in something, you will pair your belief with passion and motivation, and then, with a plan paired with massive action, nothing will stop you from achieving your goal.

One thing that differentiates me from anybody else coming into the business is no one on this planet and universe could ever look at me and say, "Jonathan, this sort of business vehicle does not work." I know it works because I grew up in it. I saw what it did for my parents. I witnessed the lifestyle they created for us and things we were able to do growing up: all the houses, all the travel, and all the best schools we attended.

And then I went and did it for myself.

My belief is 100 percent unshakable and has always been. That sort of unshakeable belief is imperative to you finding success and achieving your goals. The major things that make people quit at anything are the fears of rejection and being judged. When you have such strong belief in yourself and what you are doing, with a clear path of how you are going to achieve your goals, nothing will stop you.

Willingness to Objectively Examine Yourself

For our beliefs to be aligned, we must be willing to objectively examine ourselves, our beliefs, and our current situation. Objectively is important. Do not criticize or talk bad about yourself. There is no good, there is no bad, it is simply the truth about your current state.

We do this in a bunch of life arenas, but first and foremost we do it with our finances. We need to address where are we financially. I read that most Americans do not have $500 saved to be able to fix their car if needed.

Here are some questions to ask yourself:

- Financially, where am I today?

- Am I in debt?

- Do I have money in the bank?

- Do I live paycheck to paycheck?

- What is my current situation?

- Am I okay with that situation or do I do I want to change my situation?

If you want to change your situation, then ask:

- Where do I want to be thirty days from now?

- Where do I want to be in ninety days from now?

- Where do I want to be a year from now?

Look at yourself: how is your health? Do you have health problems? Those can make it much harder to begin your journey to achievement. Where are you spiritually in your life? Is spirituality even a part of your life? Is there something you believe in? My father used to read the *Yoga Sutras* and Buddhist philosophies. Do you participate in a more conventional sort of church?

These main areas of your life affect the way you think and the way you feel and influence your decision making. If you can objectively examine yourself and your life in these key areas and identify where you are, then you will see the limiting beliefs you hold on to. You will see the work you need to do and plan to move out of your current situation into a better one. Most importantly, you will take responsibility for your own life and realize your condition is not permanent. You alone can create something more and something better for yourself.

NINE BELIEFS THAT WE NEED TO MAKE THIS WORK

Having been in this industry generationally working in over fifty-four countries with people from all over the world, we find that these are the beliefs needed to be aligned with success in this business.

The First Belief

> Do you believe it is okay to make money? I remember sitting in meetings with my father and him asking this question, one I thought was ridiculous because, of course, everybody needs to make money, right? You must be able to make money to survive.

> I have been to areas in different countries where they believe it is okay to make money but don't believe it is okay to make a lot of it. A well-off dentist said this to

me when I was living in Denmark for the first time. I was shocked because I did not believe people believed these things. I was informed that making a lot of money is seen as trying to show off. If the beliefs that it is okay to make money and it is okay to make a lot of money are not aligned, that could inhibit your success on your journey in this networking business.

It is not about the money; it never is. It is about what we do with the money. Money is energy, but with that energy comes freedom. If you know you can be freer by having more money, does that help resolve the belief that you do not believe it is okay to make money?

The Second Belief

Do you believe that leverage income is the best way to make money?

Would you rather have money all at once or would you rather have a little over a long period of time? There is a phenomenal example of the penny doubling over time. You can see what happens if you accept a lump sum or accept the penny doubling over a year and what that ends up being. And that is wild.

Do you believe in leverage income, that mechanism of wealth we use in this business as opposed to trading time for money? By leveraging other people's time and energy together, everybody wins a little bit. Do you believe it is better to be able to create generational wealth if that is what you would like for your family, or do you think that you are taking advantage of people? Do you believe you are holding on to that negative self-limiting belief? Then you must address why you feel that way.

- ○ Are you partnered with a company that has integrity, which has real products that are patented and proprietary and effective with clinicals behind them?

- ○ Do you have a good product? Are you proud of what you share with your friends or your family or to customers?

- ○ Do you believe that their compensation package is legitimate and capped at the right levels and that new people can come into the business and make money?

All those things must be evaluated so that you can then have that belief resolved.

The Third Belief

Do you believe this networking business is the best way to make money?

There is a saying: *The wealthiest and the most successful people in the world build a network; everyone else goes and looks for work.*

This is the difference between trading time for money and leveraging the mechanics of wealth. Ask yourself:

○ Do you believe networking is the best way to make money, or do you believe you are trying to scam people into something?

○ If so, then what is causing that belief?

○ Are you partnered with the wrong company?

○ Are you doing shady practices?

○ Do you not believe in the products?

○ Do you not believe in the people with whom you are working?

You must break it down so you can address that belief. When these beliefs are aligned, then you can have success.

The Fourth Belief

Do you believe the company you have partnered with on your networking journey is the best platform company to connect with, monetize, network with, and achieve wealth with?

There are plenty of questions you should ask yourself when partnering with a company.

- ○ Have you done your due diligence?

- ○ Have you investigated who founded the company?

- ○ Is it publicly traded?

- ○ Are new people coming in and making money today?

- ○ Do they have real and effective products?

- ○ Do they have clinical studies behind those products?

- ○ Do they have a compelling compensation package that can give you residual income so you can create a massive network around the world once and then never have to do it again and reap the benefits of the network for the rest of your life, your kids' lives, their kids' lives?

- ○ Are you partnered with a company like that, and do you believe in that company?

The Fifth Belief

Do you believe that the people you are working with give you the best leadership and the best training for you to achieve your goal? You should believe 100 percent that the people you are working with to do presentations and that you bring people to see are teaching you to use the technology to generate more customers effectively.

Do you believe they are the best at it for you? If not, then you will always be distracted by looking around in the industry at what others are doing, what is over there, what is the new shiny light getting pushed. You never will fully commit to your goals because you do not believe 100 percent that you are doing it the best way possible.

My father said you can measure that. You can measure if you are doing it the best way possible, and if you are having success in the business, and that is by how much your check is, how much money you make. That is the only indication of whether you are doing it right and having success or not. Your check—you can see it. If you are not making money and you are struggling, then you must change something.

My father always told me, "If you do ten presentations, and ten people say no to you, you are doing something wrong." You must go back and find out what are you doing wrong and where you're messing up, so that your beliefs are aligned.

The Sixth Belief

Do you believe that this networking business can give you generational wealth? Do you believe that it is possible, or do you think that is some pipe dream that nobody ever gets right? What does generational wealth mean to you? What is the dollar number, what is that amount mean?

I am living proof that this sort of business, this networking business, this platform revolution business, can create generational wealth, and that when your beliefs are in line nothing will stop you. If you want to go out there and create something for your kids and their future, I can say with my heart and my head that this is an incredible vehicle you can use to potentially achieve that.

The Seventh Belief

Do you believe in yourself so that you can reach the highest level of the compensation plan, reach the highest title? Do you believe that about yourself? Can you be the number one entrepreneur in the world? Do you believe you can be that? If not, why? Because if it is not going to be you, it is going to be somebody else, so why not you? Once you have aligned with the belief that you can reach the top of the compensation package and make the most money, then it helps you to progress further on your journey to being successful in the business.

The Eighth Belief

Do you believe 100 percent in your heart and mind that you can contribute to peoples' lives in a positive and meaningful way and leave the world a better place than you found it? If you believe you can contribute to peoples' lives in a positive and meaningful way and leave the world a better place than you found it, then you will never feel like you are harassing somebody.

Instead of feeling that it is a selfish endeavor—a quota needing filled—your efforts become a contributing endeavor. You are contributing to other peoples' lives in a positive way. It is a different head space that allows you to, believe it or not, attract more people to you and what you are doing.

People do not care about what you want. People do not care about checks. People do not care about your lifestyle, your car, or your houses. They care about themselves and how their life will be impacted by what is contributed to them. When you believe you are contributing to peoples' lives, it takes you one more step further toward achieving success in this business.

The Ninth Belief

Do you believe that your past does not equal your future? Again, your past does not equal your future, meaning your background or education level does not matter. Your work experience does not matter nor what trials and tribulations you have had in your life—that is in the past. Your past does not define your future unless you live there and let it.

Do you believe your past is not equal to your future? Because if you do, you can find success in this business. As a caveat to that, I always tell people there are only two days a year you cannot accomplish anything. Those days are yesterday and tomorrow. The past does not matter. The only thing that matters is the present and the now. Are you willing to accept that to help align the belief that your past does not equal your future?

NOT COMPARING YOURSELF TO OTHERS

This journey is solely and exclusively yours, and it does not matter what other people achieve who are not on the journey. It is all about you. Do not compare yourself to others because all that can do is harm you and cause negative self-talk.

The Theft of Joy

Comparison is the thief of joy. When you compare yourself to others, even if you are achieving everything you want to achieve, it robs you of the fulfillment you would have otherwise had.

When I was a kid, all I wanted to do was fish with my father because I had never caught a fish before. He finally took me and my younger sister, Natalie, and bought our fishing poles. We were excited and luckily, I caught a fish. Shortly after, Natalie caught a fish. And guess what? Her fish was bigger than mine.

Suddenly I was pissed. I even started crying. Why? Because I got everything I wanted and was on cloud nine, but then my sister caught one bigger, and I was a mess. I had compared what I had done to what she had done, and what did that do? Natalie had an amazing day, but I was crying and pissed off. I had a terrible day! I got everything I wanted, but my perspective had changed and soured because I compared my experience to someone else's.

Do not do it. You are on your own journey. Some people move quickly to a lot of success. They reach goals, make a lot of money, and can do it quickly—whether through the influence they have had or the people they know—and that is okay. For other people, it takes years to find success in this business. That is okay too.

Someone else's success is not your failure. Do not compare yourself to others, especially when you are starting in the business. Do not look around at other people and think: *He is better looking than me. He is more charismatic. He can speak publicly, but I cannot. I am shy. He is more educated than me. He speaks more languages than me.*

Suddenly, you are putting yourself down without even getting in the game. You end up talking yourself out of it. In that way, comparison is the thief of joy and can be the thief of your success and happiness in general. So do not do it. Focus on making yourself 1 percent better every single day.

That's it. Do not strive for being the best. Don't think: *I want to be the best at this*, because that implies there is a finish line—that means your journey is a competition if you are going to be the best. If you focus on bettering yourself every single day, you can never lose and will stay on track to achieving whatever you set out to achieve.

The Business Is a Marathon, Not a Sprint

This business is a marathon, not a sprint, and some people can go fast, but some people take longer. No matter what, to build a solid stable foundation of customers and entrepreneurs in your network globally, it takes a lot of time, even years to build if you want to build a solid foundation.

You know, some people will come into their first or second month and have a huge check. They will think they are on top of the world and on top of the compensation plan. They will think that they won.

Suddenly, it is not stable. The money could be gone next month. They think: *Oh wow, I achieved the best. I got the highest title. I am maximizing the compensation plan,* and then without realizing that it was not a stable organization, their check drops, and they get a sour taste in their mouth.

Then they quit.

The first twelve months of your business are going to be your training because these businesses do not require any form of formal training. Most people have not even heard of these businesses. People are brought in by a friend, or somebody they know, and learn how to do it.

You learn by doing you. Basically, you get to ride the bike right away and start. Some people make a lot of mistakes, and that is normal. You will learn a lot but realize that people will reject you. Do not fear it. A *no* is not a no—it is a *not now*. Do not fear the rejection and do not let it keep you from persisting and achieving your goals. Recognize that to ride a bike, you must fall down a couple of times, and then once you learn from your mistakes, you will keep growing and winning every single day.

Fifty years from today, where will your networking business be? Where will it be a hundred years from today? Is it generational? Are your grandkids running it and working with it? Where is it?

Because so much rides on your posture in this business, you must come from a position of strength, which comes from absolute certainty in those beliefs we discussed earlier. It is your posture, which comes from your belief, that will attract people to you or drive them away.

Posture and Strength

When the beliefs we discussed earlier in this book are aligned, you should feel confident about the business you are part of and how it works. When you are contributing to other peoples' lives, you know you are leaving the world a better place than you found it, and your strength and posture in the business will be such that no one can take it away from you.

Those closest to us try their hardest to tell us we cannot do something. Why? Because to achieve anything new, we must break out of our comfort zone. Yet by testing our own comfort zone, we test the comfort zone of those around us.

You test your friends' comfort zone because you are now doing something they are not, evolving. You are changing and they may not like that. They will try to pull you back down with words, such as: *Do not do that. Stay here and stay who we know you are.* That is why they say your five closest friends will be a representation of who you are in your life.

Financially, they will have the same sort of house and the same source of income.

Choose your friends wisely.

I have always taught what my father said: *If we can prepare you for what is to come, you will not quit, even if the people you value most in your life look at you like you are a homeless person begging for food when you pitch them a business opportunity. They will make you feel awful, but will you quit when that happens?*

Do not let them take it away from you. Understand it, acknowledge it, and then move on. Saying *next* is powerful.

Also, never try to convince anybody to do business with you. Never try convincing anybody that this is for them because it is like trying to convince a pig it can fly. You can take a big potbelly pig, put some wings on the pig, dress it up, run it around, and toss it in the air a little bit, but as much as you want that pig to fly, it never will. You will piss off the pig and end up disappointed. The same happens when you try convincing anybody to do something with you.

Your posture and strength are instrumental to achieving what you want to achieve in this business. Accomplishing your goals and having the jaws of a pit bull will streamline your focus and break through brick walls until you get to where it is you want to get—with or without the people around you. When you have all your beliefs in line, that will get you to the end game—100 percent!

Conclusion

My father said the most powerful phrase in the English language is comprised of the smallest words because the words only have two letters.

If it is to be, it is up to me.

I am sharing this phrase because after you have gone through everything, I hope you are left with the sense that human potential is enormous. Whatever you set your mind to you can achieve. You are not stuck by any means. If you evaluate your current condition, take responsibility for it, and then set goals, a clear path of where you want to be will appear. The actions you need to take will become clear. There is nothing stopping you from achieving.

If you are not currently involved in a networking business and are interested in one, I hope this book has shown you the potential of what can be done and has given you the principles you need to be successful in any networking business, regardless of how time progresses.

Networking businesses are firmly grounded in human behavior and connecting with others. When you learn those principles, you can involve many people in your businesses globally. We have done it now for almost forty years in over fifty countries, and this book shares the tested principles of how you can do it for yourself for the rest of time.

Of course, as technology progresses, there will always new tools to facilitate the ease of the process, but learning these principles and sticking with them will keep you on track and accountable so you can also achieve success in your businesses.

There has never been a better time to become involved in a networking business. That is the action I would like you to take. Change always happens. With so many things changing in the world, establishing networking businesses seems to be something that constantly occurs.

Most successful entrepreneurs do not bank on only one thing.

There is another saying I learned from my father growing up: *Every entrepreneur has at least twelve irons on the fire, hoping that one of them will hit a home run.* So, if you are stuck in a job or on one path and have not diversified to look at other things, I suggest looking at other options.

What is your plan B?

Whether it is starting a new business, a new relationship, or a new fitness program, the number one excuse people make for themselves for not doing something and not acting is: *My situation is different; that will not happen to me.* So, if you are making that kind of excuse for yourself, there has never been a better time to look at other options that can benefit your life in some way.

I suggest looking into networking businesses and staying connected with us.

Make life fun. Live your life with joy and love and stay in a positive mental state. Do not let anybody steal your joy away from you, and whatever you set your mind to, have the courage to believe in yourself so you can do it—because you *can* do it. If it is not going to be you, it is going to be somebody else. So why not you?

Take the chance. Take a leap of faith. Dive into whatever it is you have always wanted to do and go for it. Have fun living your life with joy, courage, and a ton of fun.

What the mind can conceive and the heart will believe, you will achieve.

Ask forgiveness, never permission.

Next Steps

For more in-depth information on the topics discussed in this book, please visit our websites: www.axelme.com and www.jonathansexsmith.com

New programs will be launched in the near future.

Feel free to follow Jonathan:

YouTube: www.youtube.com/c/jonathansexsmith

Instagram and Facebook under his name Jonathan Sexsmith

For personal coaching and other programs, email JLS315@ yahoo.com and John56bp@gmail.com

About the Author

Jonathan is a second-generation wealth creator and one of the only examples in the networking industry of a successful transfer of a generational asset that has continued to grow and thrive for over three decades. He is known for his passion, energy, and charisma, and he has been successful in many industries.

He's a Presidential director, is part of the Twenty-Million-Dollar Circle, and has one of the largest networks in the industry worldwide. He is unique in that he knows the business model works. He created it for himself, lived it, and taught it to many all over the world in over fifty countries. He has also secured funds and connected high net-worth individuals and celebrities to projects ranging from technology to film and television.

Jonathan has appeared in Broadway musicals, commercials, and soap operas. He has performed on improv comedy stages in New York and LA and won video of the year for *Funny or Die.* He has lived all over the world, is fluent in two languages, and can converse appropriately in four languages. He can play the guitar, piano, and violin.

He has a second-degree black belt in Tae Kwon Do and has been a nationally ranked Olympic-style competitor. He is a Brazilian Jiu Jitsu black belt with the Carlson Gracie team and a collegiate ranked boxer, and he has trained in Muay Thai for over fifteen years in Singapore and Thailand. He is an NSCA-certified strength and conditioning specialist, a performance enhancement specialist, and USAW Olympic weightlifting club coach.

Jonathan has also trained personal trainers nationwide. He was a featured coach for *Self* magazine and a fitness contributor to several magazines and news channels. He has implemented programs throughout major gym chains nationwide and trained professional athletes and multiple celebrities.

Jonathan is an avid entrepreneur who is always looking for new opportunities and projects. His mission is to leave the world a better place than he found it.

www.ingramcontent.com/pod-product-compliance
Lightning Source LLC
Chambersburg PA
CBHW071504200326
41519CB00019B/5865